595

D0713529

Also By David Wagoner

POEMS

Dry Sun, Dry Wind (1953)
A Place to Stand (1958)
The Nesting Ground (1963)
Staying Alive (1966)
New and Selected Poems (1969)
Riverbed (1972)

NOVELS

The Man in the Middle (1954)
Money Money Money (1955)
Rock (1958)
The Escape Artist (1965)
Baby, Come on Inside (1968)
Where Is My Wandering Boy Tonight? (1970)
The Road to Many a Wonder (1974)

EDITED

Straw for the Fire:
   From the Notebooks of
   Theodore Roethke, 1943–63 (1972)

Sleeping in the Woods

A new book of poems by David Wagoner
is an occasion worth celebrating, and this
collection particularly so, for in it Wagoner
consolidates his earlier accomplishments
and moves on to new achievements. The
witty, novel, eloquent voice is still there—
the remarkable sensitivity to nature and all
its creatures—whether bird, or insect, or
fish—and the always subtle, always
satisfying rhythms of his verses. What is
new is a deepened awareness of truths
lying behind the rippling surfaces of
reality, the exultant assurance of the
maturing poet, an occasional sombre note
beneath the arpeggios of delight.

Sleeping in the Woods

DAVID WAGONER

INDIANA UNIVERSITY PRESS
BLOOMINGTON & LONDON

Published in Canada by Fitzhenry & Whiteside Limited, Don Mills, Ontario
Manufactured in the United States of America

Library of Congress Cataloging in Publication Data
Wagoner, David.
    Sleeping in the woods.

    Poems.
    I.Title.
PS3545.A345S5   811'.5'4   74–3617
ISBN 0–253–35345–9

For Patt, sleeping and waking, with love

Contents

III

IV   Seven Songs for an Old Voice

Acknowledgments

The Singing Lesson (1972) appeared originally in CRAZY HORSE. *Beginning* (1973), *The Vow* (1973), *Slow Country* (1973), and *At the Hemingway Memorial* (1973) appeared originally in THE SOUTHERN REVIEW. *The Bad Fisherman* (1974) and *Bonsai* (1974) appeared originally in POETRY NOW. *Talking to Barr Creek* (1974) and *Report from a Forest Logged by the Weyerhaeuser Company* (1974) appeared originally in THE HUDSON REVIEW. *The First Place* (1974), *Song for the Worst Day* (1974), and *This Is a Wonderful Poem* (1974) appeared originally in THE MILL MOUNTAIN REVIEW. *To Be Written in Braille* (1974) appeared originally in THE KANSAS CITY STAR. *Living in the Ruins* (1974), *Moving into the Garden* (1974), *An Offering for Dungeness Bay* (1974), *Muse* (1972), *Worms* (1972), *Elegy for Yards, Pounds, and Gallons* (1973), *The Boy of the House* (1974), *Litany* (1973), *For a Winter Wren* (1974), and *Prayer* (1972) appeared originally in POETRY. *The Labors of Thor* (1973), *Snake Hunt* (1973), *The Lesson* (1974), and *Trying to Pray* (1971) appeared originally in THE NEW YORKER. *Beauty and the Beast* (1974) appeared originally in WESTERN HUMANITIES REVIEW. *Unloading the Elephants* (1973) and *The Lost Street* (1974) appeared originally in HARPER'S. *Tachycardia at the Foot of the Fifth Green* (1972), *Note to a Literary Club* (1974), *Chorus from a Lost Play I and II* (1974), and *Raging* (1972) appeared originally in THE OHIO REVIEW. *Elegy for a Woman Who Remembered Everything* (1972) appeared originally in THE NEW REPUBLIC. *The Man Who Spilled Light* (1974) appeared originally in AMERICAN REVIEW. *Elegy for a Forest Clear-cut by the Weyerhaeuser Company* (1974) appeared originally in KAYAK. *Sleeping in the Woods* (1973) appeared originally in SALMAGUNDI. *Vacancy* (1973) appeared originally in MONMOUTH REVIEW. The group of poems entitled *Seven Songs for an Old Voice* (1973) appeared originally in THE VIRGINIA QUARTERLY REVIEW.

Sleeping in the Woods

The Singing Lesson

You must stand erect but at your ease, a posture
Demanding a compromise
Between your spine and your head, your best face forward,
Your willful hands
Not beckoning or clenching or sweeping upward
But drawn in close:
A man with his arms spread wide is asking for it,
A martyred beggar,
A flightless bird on the nest dreaming of flying.
For your full resonance
You must keep your inspiring and expiring moments
Divided but equal,
Not locked like antagonists from breast to throat,
Choking toward silence.

If you have learned, with labor and luck, the measures
You were meant to complete,
You may find yourself before an audience
Singing into the light,
Transforming the air you breathe—that malleable wreckage,
That graveyard of shouts,
That inexhaustible pool of chatter and whimpers—
Into deathless music.
But remember, with your mouth wide open, eyes shut,
Some men will wonder,
When they look at you without listening, whether
You're singing or dying.
Take care to be heard. But even singing alone,
Singing for nothing,
Singing to empty space in no one's honor,
Keep time: it will tell
When you must give the final end-stopped movement
Your tacit approval.

I

Beginning

By the stiff sheaves of ferns
And moss like green hoarfrost
I waded upstream on stones
The shades of ice
On a day when the half-frozen
Rain fell over rain
Through the lashed hemlocks
And the red roots of cedars streamed
Downstream, colder than nerves.
Not even winter wrens
Or dippers with sheathing eyelids
Had come to this:
The water plunged at its work
From slab to slab, alone,
Into pools moss-dark at noon.
I came to a stand of alders
As pale as my bones
And waited a dead hour
In the thawing dirt at their roots
Like them to begin again.

The Bad Fisherman

At first, I thought my heart was in it: trembling on the shore,
I cast my spinner over the green current
And felt it bump downstream on the stones, my throat pulsing
Like a cormorant's. As sure as I was standing in water,
I would take the father of all fish out of the river.

Some I hadn't dreamed I could see leaping
Again and again at the head of a long drift—
A summer run of steelhead or blackmouth salmon
Landing as loud as children diving, hazel-gray bellies
Arching beyond the reach of my line.

I'd have beginner's luck: I was sure of it,
Putting up with the unaccustomed homework
Of dropper loops and clinch knots, of threading snap-swivels
Or tracing a spidery maze of nylon back through willows
To find where I'd caught myself

Or fighting to free my lure from the low branches
After a haywire backswing. It rained, it stopped, a haze
Came out of the woods at sundown
To drink at the river, a hatch of caddis-flies
Flew downwind into the mouths of other cutthroats.

And still I kept casting and casting away,
Imagining the great trout that would lash at my hook
And put me to the spinning and thrashing labor of landing it
While we gaped at each other's terrible elements
At last after my years of barely touching the surface.

I went home in the dark with nothing,
But kept on fishing, not knowing what I'd learned
That first day out of natural clumsiness
With my shadow all over the water, my loud voice swearing,
And the unknown fish breaking beyond me.

Since then, I've held them in my hands and stared
Into that round incredulous eye gone flat, glazed over
With death, the lucid death I'd nearly forgotten
While casting around for want of something better,
And felt their sparse, cold blood warming my fingers.

I've gutted my last rainbow.
Instead, I wait and watch at the river's edge,
Sometimes for hours, empty handed,
As still as a heron, wishing for its eye
To see, only to see through the water.

Talking to Barr Creek

Under the peachleaf willows, alders, and choke cherries,
By coltsfoot, devil's club, sweet-after-death,
And bittersweet nightshade,
Like a fool, I sit here talking to you, begging a favor,
A lesson as hard and long as your bed of stones
To hold me together.
At first, thinking of you, my mind slid down like a leaf
From source to mouth, as if you were only one
Piece of yourself at a time,
As if you were nowhere but here or there, nothing but now,
One place, one measure. But you are all at once,
Beginning through ending.
What man could look at you all day and not be a beggar?
How could he take his eyes at their face-value?
How could his body
Bear its dead weight? Grant me your endless, ungrudging impulse
Forward, the lavishness of your light movements,
Your constant inconstancy,
Your leaping and shallowing, your stretches of black and amber,
Bluing and whitening, your long-drawn wearing away,
Your sudden stillness.
From the mountain lake ten miles uphill to the broad river,
Teach me your spirit, going yet staying, being
Born, vanishing, enduring.

The First Place

For a mile by green-and-gold light, wading upstream,
Uncertain of our feet in the rush and shimmer
Among the touching ferns, by our touching fingers,
And led by wren-song through alders felled by beavers,
We came to a pool flowing deep
And swift below water-striders, where shelving moss
Gave way at last to our bodies on the shore.

Then, while the rainbows leaped, she opened
The gift of her nakedness, stepped into that stream,
Into water so cold my hand lay nearly frozen
In the rippling shallows, so cold it seemed
Already ice to hold us apart forever.

But she was singing, welcoming the wonder
Of the river that held her light as her beauty,
And streaming with light, with the sun swept down
Through cedar and hemlock, we saw the beginning
As our eyes met over the water. She came ashore,
And we put our lives in our hands on a morning
That had no ending.

Yet suddenly I went plunging in without her
And felt the cold touching its blood brother:
That other cold held back in the heart's shadow
Against the day when it must fight
What it most fears: love's burning entrance. The shock
Blunted my hands and feet and threw me sidelong
In a circling eddy, buffeted by streamers
Bounding over the deeper stones, going white
As my skin while I flailed, faltered inshore
To a sandbar, numb as a half-man.

She waded toward me out of mercy
For a half-frozen lover, and we swam together
Easily as the down-winding current
Drawn from us like our breath
Till under our very eyelids, through our fingers,
Not alone, the river said, *not alone*
(Though chilling us deep as our swaying backbones),
And the small terrible fish in our bloodstreams,
In the veins of our minds' eyes, vanished
Upstream to spawn in the last place on earth
We could have hoped for: the first place.

The Vow

By the snowy owl in the fog
And the skate's egg and the toad
That sang once in our room
And the sturgeon's head and the scoter
Asleep on the shore and the sow
Snoring beyond her dugs,
By the dazed newborn lamb,
By the mockingbird and the doves
Turned out of their cages,
By herons and star-nosed moles,
By the muzzles of burros
And the young quail in your palm,
By the one-legged kinglet, the hawk
Stooped at our singing rosebush,
By the lark, by the dying turkey,
By the goats dancing for hens,
By the harbor seal beyond us
And the salmon at our feet,
I set my hand to love.

Slow Country

When you come to slow country, you will move
In the steady company
Of your hands and feet, your breath as still as a pool.
The landscape around you
Will seem as fixed as a permanent kingdom
Where the shape of the wind
Can not be found in any cloud or tree.
If your hand goes out
To a weed or a grassblade, you will have hours to spare
To wonder how it has come to be
(Before your fingers break it) that you have nothing
Of yours to reach as deeply
Between the stones. If your watch falls from your hand,
It will not break
Until it has taken time to strike the ground;
Meanwhile, you may follow it
And feel as detached as a true lord of the land
When it shatters in glassy splendor:
You will measure everything equally well thereafter.
Even spilled water
Will seem as placid and ornate as ice.
All your dear enemies,
Both real and imagined, will wait in their hiding places,
Waver, then float toward you,
More and more clearly known by sun- and moonlight;
They will never reach you
Except as shrinking familiars, ripe with age.
It will seem useless
To shout in the prolonged air, since you will notice
Even a scream has a beginning,
An expansive middle, and a hapless ending
Around which the silence
Has grown more calm than ever. Between your lips
And your tongue, a sweetness;
Between your lurching heart and your wits, a passage.

Stay there. You will have time
Between the dream of embracing and the full embrace
To find your love
Lying beneath you like the willing earth,
Neither turning nor falling.

To Be Written in Braille

This is not for our eyes:
They may wander, restless,
Too far from us,
Led astray by shadows.

This is not for our ears:
We are poor listeners
In that strange distress
Following all whispers.

But for our fingers:
Love, touch these silent arbors
And their dark flowers.
All of them are yours.

Song for the Worst Day

It has come shambling
Out of the mountains, the unwelcome daylight,
The ravenous morning.
What can it do but gnaw us both to the bone
By the red of evening?
Love, sing to survive this stripping away,
This terrible searching.
Sing something to be left in the long night,
To bring to nothing.

Living in the Ruins

The tyranny of doors swung shut and bolted
Against a knock or the scratching darkness
Has ended with these breaks in your walls
Where anything may leave or enter
As the moon and the wind decide. The ceiling
Has settled comfortably across the floor;
The stairways have faltered
Like waterfalls whose careless water
Is falling as far as all split-level living
To its logical conclusion in rubble.

Lean at a window now and feel no longing
For all that lay out of reach: it will reach you
Simply, uncalled-for, here in this open season,
And you must take what comes to your windowsill
To make itself at home, while broken glass
Blooms where the iris was.

What happens naturally is the advent of moss
Turning these stones to sand, establishing
The separation of powers with its rootless searching.
You have nothing to be coveted but your life:
Tending a fire to make your share of the weather
And living in these ruins to reconnoitre
Your strangest neighbor: night falling around you.

Moving into the Garden

Moving into the garden, we settle down
Between the birdbath and the hollyhocks
To wait for the beginning, leaving behind
The house we served for the best years of its life,
Making ourselves at home by the grass spider's
Hollow-throated nest in the ivy.

We have much to learn, such as what to do all day
In the rain that leans the roses against us
And how to follow all night the important paths
Of snails and shy leaf-rollers and lace bugs
And what to make of ourselves among them
At dawn when the cold light touches our fingers

That are no longer thinking of uprooting
Or pruning or transplanting but following
This fall the columbine and bleeding heart
Darkening together, the maidenhair
Closing away like all perennials,
Hardy or delicate, and turning under.

We lift handfuls of earth (is it motherly
Now? was it once? will it be again?)
And wait for the brambles to rise over the slope
Beside us like slow green breakers striking a seawall
To join with us, to mingle with what we love,
With what we've gathered here against the winter.

An Offering for Dungeness Bay

1

The tern, his lean, slant wings
Swivelling, lifts and hovers
Over the glassy bay,
Then plunges suddenly into that breaking mirror,
Into himself, and rises, bearing silver
In his beak and trailing silver
Falling to meet itself over and over.

2

Over the slow surf
Where the moon is opening,
Begin, the plover cries,
And beyond the shallows
The far-off answer,
Again, again, again,
Under the white wind
And the long boom of the breakers
Where the still whiter branches
Lie pitched and planted deep,
Only begin, the water says,
And the rest will follow.

3

Dusk and low tide and the sanderlings
Alighting in their hundreds by the last of the light
On seawrack floating in the final ripples
Lightly, scarcely touching, and now telling
This night, *Here,* and this night coming,
Here, where we are, as their beaks turn down and thin,
As fine as sandgrains, *Here is the place.*

4

The geese at the brim of darkness are beginning
To rise from the bay, a few at first in formless
Clusters low to the water, their black wings beating
And whistling like shorebirds to bear them up, and calling
To others, to others as they circle wider
Over the shelving cove, and now they gather
High toward the marsh in chevrons and echelons,
Merging and interweaving, their long necks turning
Seaward and upward, catching a wash of moonlight
And rising further and further, stretching away,
Lifting, beginning again, going on and on.

II

Muse

Cackling, smelling of camphor, crumbs of pink icing
Clinging to her lips, her lipstick smeared
Halfway around her neck, her cracked teeth bristling
With bloody splinters, she leans over my shoulder.
Oh my only hope, my lost dumfounding baggage,
My gristle-breasted, slack-jawed zealot, kiss me again.

The Labors of Thor

Stiff as the icicles in their beards, the Ice Kings
Sat in the great cold hall and stared at Thor
Who had lumbered this far north to stagger them
With his gifts, which (back at home) seemed scarcely human.

"Immodesty forbids," his sideman Loki
Proclaimed throughout the preliminary bragging
And reeled off Thor's accomplishments, fit for Sagas
Or a seat on the bench of the gods. With a sliver of beard

An Ice King picked his teeth: "Is he a drinker?"
And Loki boasted of challengers laid out
As cold as pickled herring. The Ice King offered
A horn-cup long as a harp's neck, full of mead.

Thor braced himself for elbow and belly room
And tipped the cup and drank as deep as mackerel,
Then deeper, reaching down for the halibut
Till his broad belt buckled. He had quaffed one inch.

"Maybe he's better at something else," an Ice King
Muttered, yawning. Remembering the boulders
He'd seen Thor heave and toss in the pitch of anger,
Loki proposed a bout of lifting weights.

"You men have been humping rocks from here to there
For ages," an Ice King said. "They cut no ice.
Lift something harder." And he whistled out
A gray-green cat with cold, mouseholey eyes.

Thor gave it a pat, then thrust both heavy hands
Under it, stooped and heisted, heisted again,
Turned red in the face and bit his lip and heisted
From the bottom of his heart—and lifted one limp forepaw.

Now pink in the face himself, Loki said quickly
That heroes can have bad days, like bards and beggars,
But Thor of all mortals was the grossest wrestler
And would stake his demigodhood on one fall.

Seeming too bored to bother, an Ice King waved
His chilly fingers around the mead-hall, saying,
"Does anyone need some trifling exercise
Before we go glacier-calving in the morning?"

An old crone hobbled in, foul-faced and gamy,
As bent in the back as any bitch of burden,
As gray as water, as feeble as an oyster.
An Ice King said, "She's thrown some boys in her time."

Thor would have left, insulted, but Loki whispered,
"When the word gets south, she'll be at least an ogress."
Thor reached out sullenly and grabbed her elbow,
But she quicksilvered him and grinned her gums.

Thor tried his patented hammerlock takedown,
But she melted away like steam from a leaky sauna.
He tried a whole Nelson: it shrank to half, to a quarter,
Then nothing. He stood there, panting at the ceiling,

"Who got me into this demigoddiness?"
As flashy as lightning, the woman belted him
With her bony fist and boomed him to one knee,
But fell to a knee herself, as pale as moonlight.

Bawling for shame, Thor left by the back door,
Refusing to be consoled by Loki's plans
For a quick revision of the Northodox Version
Of the evening's deeds, including Thor's translation

From vulnerable flesh and sinew into a dish
Fit for the gods and a full apotheosis
With catches and special effects by the sharpest gleemen
Available in an otherwise flat season.

He went back south, tasting his bitter lesson
Moment by moment for the rest of his life,
Believing himself a pushover faking greatness
Along a tawdry strain of misadventures.

Meanwhile, the Ice Kings trembled in their chairs
But not from the cold: they'd seen a man hoist high
The Great Horn-Cup that ends deep in the ocean
And lower all Seven Seas by his own stature;

They'd seen him budge the Cat of the World and heft
The pillar of one paw, the whole north corner;
They'd seen a mere man wrestle with Death herself
And match her knee for knee, grunting like thunder.

Beauty and the Beast

Men wept when they saw her breasts, squinted with pain
At her clear profile, boggled at her knees,
Turned slack-jawed at her rear-view walking away,
And every available inch of her hair and skin
Had been touched by love poems and delicious gossip.
The most jaundiced and jaded people in the village
Agreed with the Prince: young Beauty was a beauty.

But through the long day he doused and plucked his roses,
Drained and refilled his moat, or caulked his dungeons,
And all night long he clocked the erring planets,
Pondered the lives of saints like a Latin-monger,
Or sat up half-seas over with sick falcons,
While Beauty lingered in her sheerest nightgowns
With the light behind her, wilting from sheer boredom.

"You're a bore!" she said. "Prince Charming is a bore!"
She cried to the gaping seamstresses and fishwives.
"He's a bore!" she yelled to the scullions and butcher's helpers.
"That tedious, bland, preoccupied, prickling Princeling
Is a bore's bore!" she told the bloody barbers
And waxy chandlers leaning out to watch her
Dragging her rear-view home to Mother and Father.

But deep in the woods, behind a bush, the Beast
Had big ideas about her. When she slipped by,
Hiking her skirts to give her legs free sway
And trailing a lovely, savage, faint aroma
Fit to unman a beast, the Beast said, "Beauty,
Come live with me in the bushes where it's chancy,
Where it's scare and scare alike, where it's quick and murky."

She looked him over. Though the light was patchy,
She could see him better than she wanted to:
Wherever men have skin, the Beast had hair;
Wherever men have hair, he had black bristles;
Wherever men have bristles, he grew teeth;
And wherever men have teeth, his snaggling tusks
Lapped over his smile. So Beauty said, "No thank you."

"You'd be a sweet relief. I'd gorge on you.
I'm sick of retching my time with hags and gorgons.
You're gorgeous. Put down my rising gorge forever."
She remembered her mother whispering: *The Beast
Is a bargain. It's a well-known fact that, later,
He turns into a Prince, humble and handsome,
With unlimited credit and your father's mustache.*

*So all you have to do is grin and bear him
Till the worst is over.* But Beauty felt uncertain.
Still, after the Prince, it seemed like now or never,
And maybe all men were monsters when they saw her,
And maybe the ugliest would teach her sooner.
Her heart felt colder than a wizard's whistle:
She said, "Poor Beast, how can I say I love you?"

With horny fingers caressing everything
Available on the little world of her body,
The Beast then took her gently, his rich odor
Wafting about them like the mist from graveyards,
And Beauty began to branch out like a castle
Taller than trees, and from the highest tower
She loosened her long hair, and the Beast climbed it.

When he was spent, he lay beside her, brushing
Leaves from her buttresses, and said, "I love you."
She shrank back to herself and felt afraid.
"You'll change into something much more comfortable
Now that you've taken me," she said. "I know:
You'll be transformed to someone like Prince Charming."
"I'm always like this," he said, and drooled a little.

"If you're going to change, change now," she told him, weeping.
"Peel off that monster suit and get it over."
"I wear myself out, not in," he said. "I'll love you
In all the worst ways, as clumsily as heaven."
"Thank God," she said. And Beauty and the Beast
Stole off together, arm in hairy arm,
And made themselves scarce in the bewitching forest.

Unloading the Elephants

Out of the sliding doors
Of steel-gray boxcars
The trunks come groping
Through the gray morning.
Where are we now?
The greatest show
Is on earth, trumpeting
Down the steep ramps and bracing
Forelegs against the heavy
Heavenly bodies
They so carefully balance
Like the commandments
Shouted to massive heads, to ears
Pondering old orders,
Older than canvas.
Why are you keeping us?
In a huge row, seventeen
Elephants. *Why must we learn
From you? What have we done
To be so weighted down?*
Trunks raised, they shuffle forward
To the long parade.

Snake Hunt

On sloping, shattered granite, the snake man
From the zoo bent over the half-shaded crannies
Where rattlesnakes take turns out of the sun,
Stared hard, nodded at me, then lunged
With his thick gloves and yanked one up like a root.

And the whole hillside sprang to death with a hissing
Metallic chattering rattle: they came out writhing
In his fists, uncoiling from daydreams,
Pale bellies looping out of darker diamonds
In the shredded sunlight, dropping into his sack.

As I knelt on rocks, my blood went cold as theirs.
One snake coughed up a mouse. I saw what a mouse
Knows, as well as anyone: there, beside me,
In a cleft a foot away from my braced fingers,
Still in its coils, a rattler stirred from sleep.

It moved the wedge of its head back into shadow
And stared at me, harder than I could answer,
Till the gloves came down between us. In the sack,
Like the disembodied muscles of a torso,
It and the others searched among themselves

For the lost good place. I saw them later
Behind plate-glass, wearing their last skins.
They held their venom behind wide-open eyes.

Worms

When the spade turns over, the worms
In their sheared gangways, turning tail, go thin
Among clods or blunt out in the open,
Half-hitching in fishermen's knots and flinching
At sunlight, the pulsing line of their hearts
Strung out to be abandoned, sinking backward
And forward among the roots, like them,
Like elvers in seaweed, mouthing the darkness,
All taken in by the darkness of their mouths.

At the Hemingway Memorial

KETCHUM, IDAHO

The day's bone dry. I've come through Sun Valley
To sit beside your rock and your greening bust
Above the Big Lost River
Where sage and bitterbush and broom
Have held their own, where the cicadas
Chirr through the cottonwoods in the dead of summer.

The plaque says you're a part of this forever,
Especially the "high blue windless skies" of the Sawtooths,
And looking at big lost Papa's place,
I believe it. The road's as hard,
As shimmering, straight, and spare as early you.
The style is still the man when it deserts him.

By my foot, the husk of a cicada nymph
Lies pale as straw—the nervelessly crouched legs,
The head hunched forward hunting for some way out,
The claws grown stiff defending the clenched hollow,
The back split open,
And nothing but nothing to be brave about.

Tachycardia at the Foot of the Fifth Green

My heart is flapping away from me
As I sprawl, pushing down daisies in the fairway,
At the lambing end of March, my chin
And my lips gone numb as the sunshine.

Because I have no one here (or is it *nothing?*)
To put in charge of my breath, I struggle
Not to pass out, afraid of finding myself
Unable to dream for a last time,

Or, as now, for the first time since I was two,
Unable to stand up for fear of falling.
The next threesome or twosome will see me lying
One on a short par-four and wonder

Whether some crazy or escaping lover
Has given up the serious part of his game
To bed down by a sandtrap, keeping his eye on clouds
Instead of the ball or the flag.

Will I seem just a temporary hazard
Like casual water, to be played around?
Frogs croak. A red-tailed hawk
And a marsh hawk have flown by, bearing their names.

I hear a white-crowned sparrow's brilliant announcement,
But then some warbler, nameless, exasperating,
Reminds me how little I recognize
With or without my wits, how dimly I listen.

If my body's guest isn't thrown off the course
For this unplayable lie, I'll live to learn
What species each of us is. My ball nestles beside me
Inert and unlikely, like a marble egg.

Elegy for a Woman Who Remembered Everything

She knew the grades of all her neighbors' children, the birthdays
Of cousins once removed, the addresses of friends who had moved
Once at least—to the coordinates of cemeteries
Where their choice views lay over their front feet.

If it had a name or a number, she missed nothing:
A mailman's neck size, the unpronounceable village where the
                                                        dentist's
Wife's half-sister ruined her kneecap, an almanac of sutures,
The ingredients of five thousand immemorial crocks.

Her ears were as perfectly pitched as a piano-tuner's.
In the maze of total recall, she met with amazement
The data of each new day, absorbed the absorbing facts and the
                                                        absorbent
Fictions of everyone's life but her own, losing the thread

Of that thin tracery in dialogue hauled back verbatim
Through years leaning cracked and crooked against each other.
Death, you may dictate as rapidly or incoherently as you wish:
She will remember everything about you. Nothing will escape her.

The Man Who Spilled Light

The man who spilled light wasn't to blame for it.
He was in a hurry to bring it home to the city
Where, everyone said, there was too much darkness:
"Look at those shadows," they said. "They're dangerous.
Who's there? What's that?" and crouching, "Who are *you*?"
So he went and scraped up all the light he could find.

But it was too much to handle and started spilling:
Flakes and star-marks, shafts of it splitting
To ring-light and light gone slack or jagged,
Clouds folded inside out, whole pools
And hummocks and domes of light,
Egg-light, light tied in knots or peeled in swatches,
Daylight as jumbled as jackstraws falling.

Then everything seemed perfectly obvious
Wherever they looked. There was nothing they couldn't see.
The corners and alleys all looked empty,
And no one could think of anything terrible
Except behind their backs, so they all lined up
With their backs to walls and felt perfectly fine.
And the man who'd spilled it felt fine for a while,
But then he noticed people squinting.

They should have been looking at everything, and everything
Should have been perfectly clear, and everyone
Should have seemed perfectly brilliant, there was so much
Dazzle: people were dazzled, they were dazzling,
But they were squinting, trying to make darkness
All over again in the cracks between their eyelids.
So he swept up all the broken light
For pity's sake and put it back where it came from.

Elegy for Yards, Pounds, and Gallons

A duly concocted body of our elders
Is turning you out of office and schoolroom
Through ten long years, is phasing you
Out of our mouths and lives forever.

Words have been lost before: some hounded
Nearly to death, and some transplanted
With roots dead set against stone,
And some let slide into obscure senescence,

Some even murdered beyond recall like extinct animals—
(It would be cruel to rehearse their names:
They might stir from sleep on the dusty shelves
In pain for a moment).

Yet you, old emblems of distance and heaviness,
Solid and liquid companions, our good measures,
When have so many been forced to languish
For years through a deliberate deathwatch?

How can we name your colorless replacements
Or let them tell us for our time being
How much we weigh, how short we are,
Or how little we have left to drink?

Goodbye to Pounds by the Ton and all their Ounces,
To Gallons, Quarts, and Pints,
To Yards whose Feet are inching their last Mile,
Weighed down, poured out, written off,

And drifting slowly away from us
Like drams, like chains and gills,
To become as quaint as leagues and palms
In an old poem.

Note to a Literary Club

RACINE—*The Middleport Literary Club met Wednesday afternoon at the country home of Mrs. Thereon Johnson near Racine. Mrs. Roy Cassell reviewed a book of poetry titled "Riverbed" by David Wagoner. Mrs. Cassell read excerpts from the volume . . . that displayed the simplicity of his poetry.*

ATHENS (OHIO) MESSENGER, APRIL 30, 1973

When ladies read poems in the heart of Ohio
On April afternoons under heady trellises,
They see them clearly, simply,
And naturally, having been born there, I did too,
Displaying signs of simplicity even at age five
By reciting a poem (taught me by a well-meaning lady)
Beside a red-plush Presbyterian pulpit
About a bog and a bullfrog
And a grumpy boy on a bumpy log
Learning to say *Cheer-up, cheer-up.*
It all seemed plain and painless to me then,
But now, when I know even more frog-songs by heart,
I try to honor those masters of emphatic repetition
In still more simple ways.

Ladies, cheer up. How can you and I go wrong
Gathering once more by any riverbed
Where something as good as frogs has been known to happen
Once in a great while? I thank you kindly
For your kind of attention. But a word of caution:
I know five poets who escaped from Ohio
And five more who went there on purpose, intending to spawn.
You may be hearing them croak at any moment.

The Boy of the House

Mother, this morning when I woke
My head stayed undercover.
It didn't get up when I got up.
It said the game was over.

It said if I had to wash a face
To go scout up another
And knife-and-fork a different mouth.
Mother, what's the matter?

The dog hides under the leaky sink.
The cat has swiped its tongue.
What do they know that I don't know?
I think there's something wrong.

The milk has turned. The vacuum bag
Is full of long white hairs,
And what perks up in the coffeepot
Has been dripping down for years.

And what comes out of the picture tube
Is spilling on the carpet.
It's spreading over Father's shoes
As thick as rainbow sherbet.

He's blinking one of his eyes again
Sixty times a minute.
His hands are locked below his chin.
His chin has relish on it.

His toes are aiming left and right.
His nose is pointing up.
Mother, I hear his stomach growl
Like a watchdog at a pup.

Go look behind his socks and shorts,
Borrowed, old, and blue.
You'll find a book with a broken back:
What Every Boy Should Know.

The freezer growls in its gamy room,
Guarding parts of cows,
And through the pounding door I see
Jehovah's Witnesses.

Mother, before I spoil myself,
I'm going back to bed.
I don't mind losing at playing house,
But I mustn't lose my head.

Whoever let me out last night
Forgot to punch my ticket.
My head butts into my pillow now
Like a ram into a thicket.

Litany

Our Sister of the Disposable Dolls and Doilies
    (Who was a bride and might have danced again),
        Remember us among your souvenir pillows
            At the hearth of your heart beside the broken wishbones.
Our Brother of Safety Glass and Belted Nylons
    (Who was a groom and should have served again),
        Enlarge us in glossies, bear our black-and-whiteness
            By the bridges, lifts, and trusses of the night.
Our Daughters and Sons of the Saturated Fat
    (Who were nothing once and might have been again),
        Blame us as far afield as kissing cousins,
            Dead hussies and cads with unencumbered chattels.
Our Lady of Royal Jelly and Foot Cream
    (Who should have had salvation and may again),
        Take us spun-dry or awash, our bilges empty,
            And the salt-free ocean permanently pressed.
Our Father of the Slice and the Instant Transplant
    (Who had to be sworn in and suborned again),
        Forgive us our wakes and watches, turn us right
            Like dimmer-switches and thermostats at daybreak.
Our Ghost of the Clean Vacated Premises
    (Who was and is and never shall be again),
        Dispose us among the tone-deaf multitudes.
        Blink at our tears. Shine on our shrinking pupils.

III

This is a Wonderful Poem

Come at it carefully, don't trust it, that isn't its right name,
It's wearing stolen rags, it's never been washed, its breath
Would look moss-green if it were really breathing,
It won't get out of the way, it stares at you
Out of eyes burnt gray as the sidewalk,
Its skin is overcast with colorless dirt,
It has no distinguishing marks, no I.D. cards,
It wants something of yours but hasn't decided
Whether to ask for it or just take it,
There are no policemen, no friendly neighbors,
No peacekeeping busybodies to yell for, only this
Thing standing between you and the place you were headed,
You have about thirty seconds to get past it, around it,
Or simply to back away and try to forget it,
It won't take no for an answer: try hitting it first
And you'll learn what's trembling in its torn pocket.
Now, what do you want to do about it?

Chorus from a Lost Play   I

Again, we sing of man, the buckler of wind,
Tide-lifter, fire-stalker, ingenious crammer,
Inventor of death masks, nearsighted diver,
Proud maker of anthems to himself on sheepskin.

Where will his tongue not wag or his mind wander?
And what will he not take with his light fingers?
And who shall deny his birthright of safe plunder?
Has he not written in blood *I am the Master?*

Was he not born to meddle and mar forever?
Consider his majesty both standing and sitting:
His clever fingers hide from one another,
His bulging forehead broods on the world's egg.

Count his hard bargains, this plum-pruning grafter,
This flower-forcing gnome, sweet poisoner,
This keeper of blades, red-fingered sharpener.
What overlord can snatch away his laurel?

See him again careering through the country,
Outnumbered by the senses of other kingdoms:
The wary animals, sly vegetables,
And thick-veined minerals unearthed, unearthly.

Now see him stand at last in the barren valley
Surrounded by heaps of whalebone and plucked feathers,
By husks and roots from the dry pits of heaven.
Believer, worshipper, come close to touch him.

In the name of God, he'll dry your tears and kill you.

Chorus from a Lost Play   II

Pity the masterless man. He lies by the road
Under our shade trees, neither coming nor going.
He folds his arms. He sits down by our river
Watching wild birds alight in the evening.

He sleeps and eats as he may and stoops to nothing.
He speaks before he is spoken to. He stares
When he should bow. He will not come when he's called.
Though arrows point the way, he will not follow.

Haven't we offered him our choicest masters
Who wear brave hats, who stamp themselves on silver,
Who preside in rooms with guards at every window
Commanding views that overlook our city?

How lonely to have no orders! How terrible
To bed down under a moon swelling and shrinking!
He keeps no schedules, suffers no opinions.
He has given up, yet he will not surrender.

Our clappers and gongs and sirens call to him;
He will not answer. Clockless and careless dreamer,
He pledges allegiance to unsanctioned demons
Housed in himself and disregards our fathers.

What can he do or be? Pity him. Damn him.

Report from a Forest
Logged by the Weyerhaeuser Company

Three square miles clear-cut.
Now only the facts matter:
The heaps of gray-splintered rubble,
The churned-up duff, the roots, the bulldozed slash,
The silence,

And beyond the ninth hummock
(All of them pitched sideways like wrecked houses)
A creek still running somewhere, bridged and dammed
By cracked branches.
No birdsong. Not one note.

And this is April, a sunlit morning.
Nothing but facts. Wedges like halfmoons
Fallen where saws cut over and under them
Bear ninety or more rings.
A trillium gapes at so much light.

Among the living: a bent huckleberry,
A patch of salal, a wasp,
And now, making a mistake about me,
Two brown-and-black butterflies landing
For a moment on my boot.

Among the dead: thousands of fir seedlings
A foot high, planted ten feet apart,
Parched brown for lack of the usual free rain,
Two buckshot beercans, and overhead,
A vulture big as an eagle.

Selective logging, they say, we'll take three miles,
It's good for the bears and deer, they say,
More brush and berries sooner or later,
We're thinking about the future—if you're in it
With us, they say. It's a comfort to say

Like *Dividend* or *Forest Management* or *Keep Out*.
They've managed this to a fare-thee-well.
In Chicago, hogs think about hog futures.
But staying with the facts, the facts,
I mourn with my back against a stump.

The Lesson

That promising morning
Driving beside the river,
I saw twin newborn lambs
Still in a daze
At the grassy sunlight;
Beyond them, a day-old colt
As light-hoofed as the mare
That swayed over his muzzle—
Three staggering new lives
Above the fingerlings
From a thousand salmon nests—
And I sang on the logging road
Uphill for miles, then came
To a fresh two thousand acres
Of a familiar forest
Clear-cut and left for dead
By sawtoothed Weyerhaeuser.

I haunted those gray ruins
For hours, listening to nothing,
Being haunted in return
By vacancy, vacancy,
Till I grew as gray as stumps
Cut down to size. They drove me
Uphill, steeper and steeper,
Thinking: the salmon will die
In gillnets and crude oil,
The colt be broken and broken,
And the lambs leap to their slaughter.

I found myself in a rage
Two-thirds up Haystack Mountain
Being buzzed and ricochetted
By a metallic whir
That jerked me back toward life
Among young firs and cedars—
By a rufous hummingbird
Exulting in wild dives
For a mate perched out of sight
And cackling over and over,
Making me crouch and cringe
In his fiery honor.

Elegy for a Forest
Clear-cut by the Weyerhaeuser Company

Five months after your death, I come like the others
Among the slash and stumps, across the cratered
Three square miles of your graveyard:
Nettles and groundsel first out of the jumble,
Then fireweed and bracken
Have come to light where you, for ninety years,
Had kept your shadows.

The creek has gone as thin as my wrist, nearly dead
To the world at the dead end of summer,
Guttering to a pool where the tracks of an earth-mover
Showed it the way to falter underground.
Now pearly everlasting
Has grown to honor the deep dead cast of your roots
For a bitter season.

Those water- and earth-led roots decay for winter
Below my feet, below the fir seedlings
Planted in your place (one out of ten alive
In the summer drought),
Below the small green struggle of the weeds
For their own ends, below grasshoppers,
The only singers now.

The chains and cables and steel teeth have left
Nothing of what you were:
I hold my hands over a stump and remember
A hundred and fifty feet above me branches
No longer holding sway. In the pitched battle
You fell and fell again and went on falling
And falling and always falling.

Out in the open where nothing was left standing
(The immoral equivalent of a forest fire),
I sit with my anger. The creek will move again,
Come rain and snow, gnawing at raw defiles,
Clear-cutting its own gullies.
As selective as reapers stalking through wheatfields,
Selective loggers go where the roots go.

Sleeping in the Woods

Not having found your way out of the woods, begin
Looking for somewhere to bed down at nightfall
Though you have nothing
But parts of yourself to lie on, nothing but skin and backbone
And the bare ungiving ground to reconcile.
From standing to kneeling,
From crouching to turning over old leaves, to going under,
You must help yourself like any animal
To enter the charmed circle
Of the night with a body not meant for stretching or sprawling:
One ear-flap at a time knuckling your skull,
Your stiff neck (needing
An owl's twist to stay even) cross-purposing your spine,
With rigid ankles, with nowhere to put your arms.
But now, lying still
At last, you may watch the shadows seeking their own level,
The ground beneath you neither rising nor falling,
Neither giving nor taking
From the dissolving cadence of your heart, identical darkness
Behind and before your eyes—and you are going
To sleep without a ceiling,
For the first time without walls, not *falling* asleep, not losing
Anything under you to the imponderable
Dead and living
Earth, your countervailing bed, but settling down
Beside it across the slackening threshold
Of the place where it is always
Light, at the beginning of dreams, where the stars, shut out
By leaves and branches in another forest, burn
At the mattering source
Forever, though a dream may have its snout half sunk in blood
And the mind's tooth gnaw all night at bone and tendon
Among the trembling snares:
Whoever stumbles across you in the dark may borrow

Your hidebound substance for the encouragement
Of mites or angels;
But whatever they can't keep is yours for the asking. Turn up
In time, at the first faint stretch of dawn, and you'll see
A world pale-green as hazel,
The chalk-green convolute lichen by your hand like sea fog,
The fallen tree beside you in half-light
Dreaming a greener sapling,
The dead twigs turning over, and your cupped hand lying open
Beyond you in the morning like a flower.
Making light of it,
You have forgotten why you came, have served your purpose, and
                                                              simply
By being here have found the right way out.
Now, you may waken.

For a Winter Wren

In the first rain after a dry summer,
Small as a leaf, the color of fallen leaves,
You sang at the foot of a fallen cedar
Like a dream of singing, more quiet,
More intricate than the mass of stems
And moss-light roots you lighted on
Where the earth still clung to the dead, a song
Gentle and distant, nearly disappearing
Under the hush of the rain,
The soft trills rising out of next to nothing
To claim this side of silence.

Bonsai

(TRANSPLANTED JANUARY 1973)

Four times before, this fir
Has turned from dirt to heaven, telling
Darkness from sunlight, stone from the gnarled air,
Rain falling from rain
Already fallen.

Its trunk, as twisted
As a root, was once a root,
Now split into five, reaching a mad balance
Against the memory of its bonsai masters:
Bulldozers, earth-movers.

Once, it was growing up-
Side down from an overhang, a stripped roadbank
Among the stumps of slaughtered and toppled others,
Wrenching itself, groping its way
Out of disaster.

Its buds are ready to burst
This spring, outward and upward, taking
One more turn between sky and a clutch of earth.
A frost-numbed bee clings to one stem
For dear life.

The Lost Street

"Just imagine: tomorrow morning you get in your car to go to work. You start to pull out of the driveway, but—no street."

What Highways Mean to You
(AUTO DEALERS TRAFFIC SAFETY COUNCIL)

You sit for a moment, idling, remembering
Another street running away from you
Before you learned to walk
Across it, even beside it: strange as a river
Under the elmtrees, it blurred
Uphill as far as the hospital
Or downhill into the dark city.

But this one, no longer stretching toward work,
Had been different, indifferent,
As easy to forget as a hall carpet
Leading from sleep to worry, from love
To bewilderment, from the steep hillside
Up to the greenhouse and the reservoir
Or down to the dimmed-out, burning city.

Now the deepening grass and brambles
Remind you there was somewhere you were going
Around the house instead of looking through glass
At this barely believable morning: you must get out
Of the car and stand on the ground,
Then kneel on it like a penitent gardener,
Touching it with your hands, crawling again to know it.

Raging

Suddenly the stone tools spilled from the racks in my forehead.
I raged in the room, wanting to fall and wrestle through the floor
To the dirt, beside myself, myselves raking the air
As shaggy as half-men in a guttering kitchen midden.

But the door creaked open. We stood still
In opposite corners, drawing enough blood
To fill the darkened corners of our eyes,
While that sweet, reasonable third self
Came in and joined us like our motherwit.

The hard air melted out
Of our mouths, flowed out the window,
And came back soft as evening.
We drank it without speaking.

Vacancy

*"We can think away objects, but
not the space which they occupy."*
EINSTEIN

The chair and table both go quietly;
The rug picks up its dust and disappears;
The floor and wallboards make room for the ceiling
To shut down on that thinker, alone at last
Among the point-blank furniture of his brain.

Do Not Write In This Space.

Trying to Pray

My voice from its poor box
Enters the rank and file
Of voices fumbling prayers
From pew to nave to chancel,
As rank as any, as grating,
But rising no further
Than the head I've bent for it.

It raises no Father
From the stained broken glass
Strewn on my mind's eye,
No Son on a crutch,
No Ghost in Day-Glo,
Not even the Horny One
Hoofing it red-faced.

Instead, I hear the thump
Of knees against stone, half-see
Out of the squeezed corners
Of my eyes those squeezed in corners
By the crosshatched light
Asking for hope or help
Or maybe enough rope.

My one-way litany
Lies burning in my palms:
Tied to itself, the Self
May mutter trust or grief
Down through its crooked cave
And swallow the echo,
But true spelunkers go
On hands as well as knees
Till, face against rock face
In the votive darkness,
They touch what will not answer.

Prayer

From this one breath,
By as many heartbeats
As my clenched fingers,
Make one inch of song.

IV

Seven Songs for an Old Voice

Fire Song

I watch the point of the twirling stick
Where you are sleeping, where you will come again.
Already your breath, pale as fog through a vine-maple,
Is rising through shreds of cedarbark toward me.
Open your dark-red eye, Fire-brother.
Here is my breath to warm you. You may have all my breath.
Show me your yellow tongue, and I will feed you
Alder and black locust in thick branches
To gnaw in half like Beaver. Now, with you beside me,
I can see the eyes of the First People staring toward us
Hungrily, with the hollow look of Soul-catchers.
Hold them out at the thin edge of darkness, and I will keep you
As long and as well as I keep myself through the night.
Toward dawn, you may lie down slowly, drift slowly out of the
                                                    ashes
To sleep again at the cold point of my spirit.

Song for the Maker of Nightmares

You start your campfire on my breast like a mad grandfather
And eat my sleep for your food. Whenever you waken,
I must redden for war with your grunting children's children—
Thorn Cheek, Skinless Foot, Old Knife at the Lips, Moss Face,
Mouth-changer No One Hears, Lost Hand, my terrible brothers.
If you fall asleep in the middle of my fear, I come back
To claim my throat and my numb belly, like a dog
Who has strayed too far at night and swallowed his voice
At the first yawning of Bear Mother. Tonight I have no charms
To make you sleep. Begin again. Call out of their burrows like
                                        woodworms
Stump, Mouse Woman, Snag, Split Man. Even in my terror
I must believe you: I will drink what you bring me in my broken
                                        skull,
The bitter water which once was sweet as morning.

Song for the Soul Going Away

I have wakened and found you gone
On a day torn loose from its moon, uprooted
And wilting. How can I call you back with dust in my mouth?
My words lie dead on the ground like leaves. Night speech,
Water speech, the speech of rushes and brambles
Have thinned to muttering and a vague crackle,
And the bird in my ribcage has turned black and silent.
Where a man would stand, I sit; where a man would sit,
I lie down burning; where a man would speak,
My voice shrinks backward into its dark hovel.
The dragonfly has taken his glitter from the pool,
Birds' eggs are stones, all berries wither.
Without you, my eyes make nothing of light and shadow,
And the cup of each eyelid has run dry.
I go as aimless as my feet among sticks and stones,
Thinking of you on your mad, bodiless journey.

Dark Song

The faint scraping of stalk against leaf, the twig
And the caught thorn not quite breaking, yielding
Slowly in the night, are nothing
To fear: nothing knows
I am in this darkness, nothing knows which way
My dangerous eyes are turned. When young,
I bit the dark and clawed it, held my knife under its deep belly,
Set fire to it, jabbed it with sticks, strutted unseeing
Through its heart to my own rescue.
Now what stands behind my back is afraid:
I wait for longer than it can wait,
Listening, moving less than shadows.
It is mine now, soft as the breath of owls.

Song for the Soul Returning

Without singing, without the binding of midnight,
Without leaping or rattling, you have come back
To lodge yourself in the deep fibres under my heart,
More closely woven than a salmonberry thicket.
I had struck the rocks in your name, but no one answered;
Left empty under the broken wings of the sun,
I had tasted and learned nothing. Now the creek no longer
Falters from stone to stone with a dead fishtailing
But bursts like the ledges of dawn, the east and west winds
Meet on the hillside, and the softening earth
Spreads wide for my feet where they have never dared to go.
Out of the silent holts of willow and hazel, the wild horses,
Ears forward, come toward us, hearing your voice rise from my
                                                        mouth.
My hands, whose craft had disappeared, search out each other
To shelter the warm world returning between them.

Song for the First People

When you learned that men were coming, you changed into rocks,
Into fish and birds, into flowers and rivers in despair of us.
The tree under which I bend may be you,
That stone by the fire, the nighthawk swooping
And crying out over the swamp reeds, the reeds themselves.
Have I held you too lightly all my mornings?
I have broken your silence, dipped you up
Carelessly in my hands and drunk you, burnt you,
Carved you, slit your calm throat and danced on your skin,
Made charms of your bones. You have endured
All of it, suffering my foolishness
As the old wait quietly among clumsy children.
Now others are coming, neither like you nor like men.
I must change, First People. How do I change myself?
If no one can teach me the long will of the cedar,
Let me become Water Dog, Bitterroot, or Shut Beak.
Change me. Forgive me. I will learn to crawl, stand, or fly
Anywhere among you, forever, as though among great elders.

Death Song

I touch the earth on all fours like a child,
And now my forehead touches the earth.
For the sake of my joys, Sleepmaker, let me in.
I have turned away from none of the six directions.
I have praised the rising and the dying wind,
Water falling or vanishing, even the end of grass.
I have welcomed the seasons equally
And been one with all weather from the wild to the silent.
The only blood left on my hands is my own: now my heart
Will be strict, admitting none, letting none go.
Close all my mouths. I will sleep inside of sleep,
Honoring the gift of darkness till it breaks.
I sing for a cold beginning.

DAVID WAGONER, editor of
Poetry Northwest, has written eight vol-
umes of poetry, including *Riverbed, The
Nesting Ground,* and *Staying Alive.* He is
editor of *Straw for the Fire: From the
Notebooks of Theodore Roethke.* His most
recent novel is *The Road to Many a
Wonder.*